EVERY MINISTRY NEEDS HELP

Robyn Gool

With Special Foreword by
Oral Roberts

EVERY MINISTRY NEEDS HELP

Published by
CONQUERORS PUBLISHING
P.O. Box 240433
Charlotte, NC 28224

Phone: (704) 527-8181
FAX: (704) 527-8515

ISBN 0-9648460-1-2

For quantity purchases please contact the publisher.

Printed in the United States of America.

CONTENTS

Foreword   5

Introduction   7

Chapter 1   EVERY MINISTRY NEEDS   11
             THE RIGHT KIND OF HELP

Chapter 2   HELP THAT KNOWS THE   20
             VOICE OF GOD

Chapter 3   HELP THAT SERVES   31
             AS UNTO THE LORD

Chapter 4   HELP THAT IS FAITHFUL   42

Chapter 5   HELP THAT IS COMMITTED   57
             TO EXCELLENCE

Chapter 6   HELP THAT HAS THE   72
             LEADER'S SPIRIT

Chapter 7   GETTING INVOLVED   82

About the Author   93

Foreword

I t pleases me very much to write the foreword to this outstanding book through which every one of us in the ministry can receive unusual help. I, like all ministers of the gospel, need special help at times. And Robyn Gool's new book is ministering to me in a profound way.

When Robyn came out of high school as one of the highest ranked tennis players in America, it was our joy that he chose Oral Roberts University for his education. He helped make ORU's tennis team rank in the top ten. Robyn stood out in his quiet way and I was drawn to him as his admirer and friend. I think it was the atmosphere of Christ's presence that pervades ORU that got hold of Robyn's heart. It was not long until God became #1 in his life and revealed to him his Higher Call.

After graduation the call of God on Robyn's life was so consuming that he laid his tennis racket down and picked up his Bible to obey his destiny as a God-called minister of the gospel — the whole gospel.

Soon he and Marilyn, his lovely wife who is a powerful preacher in her own right, were on fire for God. The Word became all-consuming in their lives and outreach. The Word preached with the anointing began to draw and win people to God. The crowds, at first small, grew until they had to have faith to build a large sanctuary that stood out in its beauty and utility, as did their ministry.

My first time to preach for Robyn was a powerful experience, a great reception, with people grounded in the Word and in the anointing. The church is aptly named, *VICTORY CHRISTIAN CENTER*. Robyn has been voted one of the top ten ministers in Charlotte and I could see the reason why.

I promise you the title of Robyn's book, *"Every Ministry Needs Help,"* is true. I know it is in my life. Every ministry needs the *right kind* of help.

I believe as you start reading this book, you won't put it down. It's that unusual and powerful with its many helps. I treasure my copy. I bless it with my prayers and faith; and you as you read, meditate and take it into your spirit.

— *ORAL ROBERTS*

Introduction

Every ministry needs help. There is not one man or woman of God who has a part in the Lord Jesus' ministry that doesn't need help.

When my wife and I began Victory Christian Center in Charlotte, we agreed together according to Matthew 18:19, that God would send us the help we needed — the right people to be in the right positions. We wanted people who were sent by the Heavenly Father.

It was beautiful and wonderful to watch our prayers unfold before our eyes. As a result, the ministry has been built and established, and is functioning on a solid foundation. The message you will find in this book has been a key in keeping church splits and a mass exodus from occurring, as well as keeping me from the discouragement and anxieties that can present themselves to pastors. To God be the glory!

However, as I began to travel across the country and to different parts of the world, I saw many pastors struggling to the point of discouragement, frustration and fatigue. As I had the opportunity to talk with them and observe their ministries it became apparent that much of this could have been avoided if the helpers in their churches had been the right kind of help.

Far too many men and women of God have simply settled for whomever wanted to volunteer or be involved, without making sure the people were ready. As a result, an organization that was meant to be vital, strong and efficient, became stagnant, divisive and hindered.

Every ministry needs help, but not just any kind of help. As you read through the pages of this book, my desire is that it will become apparent to you how you can become the right kind of help in a church or ministry.

God has assigned members of His body to specific local churches because their skills, talents, resources and abilities match the visions and calls of particular pastors. However, for a pastor to allow walk-ins or newcomers to immediately begin helping has proven to be devastating to some ministries. Persons wanting to assist may be sincere, but they may be the wrong kind of help.

If your desire is to be a blessing to the Kingdom of

God, and to strengthen your local church, I thank God this book is in your hands.

Upon completion of your reading, let me encourage you to share this book with your pastor.

Now, as we begin, let's allow the life of Moses and Jesus to introduce our study.

1

EVERY MINISTRY NEEDS THE RIGHT KIND OF HELP

E very minister needs help at some point in time. Maybe not to the extreme of death, as you will see in the case of Moses, but certainly in the depth of sincerity. Some ministers start off acting as if they can take on the world, but eventually they face reality and acknowledge that they need help. That's when the obedience of the laity kicks in, as the Chief Shepherd of the sheep orchestrates to position the body in the right church or ministries.

In Numbers 11 we find that Moses needed help. But he did not require just any help. He needed the right kind of help. He asked God, "Wherefore hast thou afflicted thy servant? and wherefore have I not found favour in thy sight, that thou layest the burden of all this people upon me?

"Have I conceived all this people? Have I begotten them, that thou shouldest say unto me, Carry them in thy bosom, as a nursing father beareth the sucking child, unto the land which thou swarest unto their fathers? Whence should I have flesh to give unto all this people? for they weep unto me, saying, Give us flesh, that we may eat. I am not able to bear all this people alone, because it is too heavy for me" (Numbers 11:11-14).

Moses was tired and fed up with their attitude. Rather than deal with the people's constant murmuring and complaining, he said he preferred that God take his life. "And if thou deal thus with me, kill me, I pray thee, out of hand, if I have found favour in thy sight; and let me not see my wretchedness" (v.15).

He was simply saying: "Lord, I need help! I'm not able to handle all these people by myself. If I can't have help, I'd rather be dead!"

The Lord replied to Moses, "Gather unto me seventy men of the elders of Israel, whom thou knowest to be the elders of the people, and officers over them; and bring them unto the tabernacle of the congregation, that they may stand there with thee" (v.16).

Help was on the way! Seventy elders would share the burden. God continued, "I will come down and talk with thee there: and I will take of the spirit which is upon thee, and will put it upon them; and they shall bear the burden of the people with thee, that thou bear it not thyself alone" (v.17).

Moses wasn't given just <u>any</u> help, but as you will see later, the right kind of help.

Jesus Needed Help

Everywhere Jesus preached, great crowds gathered. Let's look at one account recorded in the ninth and tenth chapters of Matthew. "But when he saw the multitudes, he was moved with compassion on them, because they fainted, and were scattered abroad, as sheep having no shepherd" (Matthew 9:36).

Then He said to His disciples, "The harvest truly is plenteous, but the labourers are few; Pray ye therefore the Lord of the harvest, that he will send forth laborers into his harvest" (vv. 37-38).

What did He ask them to do? Pray that laborers would be sent out. In other words, Jesus *needed* help. He knew that He could only be in one place at one time, touching only a limited number of people. Yet there were multitudes that needed His touch. So look at what He immediately did.

13

"And when he had called unto him his twelve disciples, he gave them power against unclean spirits, to cast them out, and to heal all manner of sickness and all manner of disease" (Matthew 10:1).

I can see Jesus doing this with urgency because of the vast number of people who were oppressed, tormented, spiritually dead and depraved. He was limited to time and space and needed help. In essence, when He called the twelve, He was saying:

"I'm commissioning you to go in My name. I can't do it alone!"

At the feeding of the five thousand, the Lord didn't say to the twelve, "Watch and see what I am about to do!" No, He involved them in the process. "And he said to his disciples, Make them sit down by fifties in a company" (Luke 9:14).

Who arranged the seating? The *disciples.*

Then Christ "took the five loaves and the two fishes, and looking up to heaven, he blessed them, and brake, and gave to the disciples to set before the multitude" (v.16).

Who fed the five thousand? The *disciples.* Christ did the praying, but the miracle was in their hands. Every time they broke off a piece of bread, it kept multiplying.

As the ministry grew, Jesus realized He would need

the help of even more than the twelve disciples. "After these things the Lord appointed other seventy also, and sent them two and two before his face into every city and place, whither he himself would come" (Luke 10:1).

Again, He said, "The harvest truly is great, but the laborers are few" (v.2). Then He gave them power and authority to preach and minister to the needs of the people.

Jesus had a *Helps Ministry.* Just before the Last Supper, He sent Peter and John, saying, "Go and prepare us the Passover, that we may eat" (Luke 22:8).

He told them where they would meet a man who would lead them to the house where the Passover would be observed. And remember, it was Peter and John who made the preparations.

Throughout Scripture you will find the same pattern. Elijah was aided by Elisha. Paul was assisted by Timothy. These people were involved in *helping* until God launched them into their own respective ministries.

The Church Needs Help

I am a graduate of Oral Roberts University. And I can vividly remember Oral Roberts' candid address to our incoming freshman class. He told us that because we had willingly chosen ORU and had not been forced to come, we were expected to be an asset and a blessing. He warned us that if at any time we were deemed problematic, the administration would gladly help us to find our way back home.

There are a lot of church members who need to find their way to other churches, because they are not willing to conform, nor comply, and they are neither flexible, nor adaptable. They're simply a part of the problem.

Yet, if we pool our resources, gifts and strengths in whatever ministry or church we are in, we can accomplish the will of God more quickly and make an impact in our cities, states, nation and world.

The Ministry of Helps is God's plan for every believer at some point in his or her life. The Word says, "From whom the whole body fitly joined together and compacted by that which every joint supplieth, according to the effectual working in the measure of every part, maketh increase of the body unto the edifying of itself in love" (Ephesians 4:16).

God knows how to assemble His body. He knows the special place where you belong and the particular ministry to which you've been called. Your gifts and talents are unique. "Now you are the body of Christ, and members in particular" (1 Corinthians 12:27).

The eye can't say to the hand, "I don't have need of you." The foot can't say to the arm, "You're not really necessary!"

Every individual is needed in the body of Christ. You have valuable tools, insights, gifts and abilities that will fit into your local church like crucial pieces of a puzzle. Each individual part completes the total picture.

The abilities you possess were given to you for a purpose. God never intended for them to be hidden, but to be set into motion.

Becoming God's Instrument

If you listen, you will hear the Lord telling you, "I have brought you to this ministry because it has a vision that coincides with the gifts and talents I have given you." You and the ministry are to become one.

The helps ministry is comprised of people who are fitly joined together by Christ to hold up the arms of the person whom God has placed in leadership.

It should be the passion of every Christian to be used of the Lord. If that is your desire, you must be willing to say, "Lord, *please change me* to be a person you can truly use."

Yes, you must be ready to be molded, shaped, nurtured, developed — even rebuked and corrected into the instrument God wants you to become.

Every ministry needs help, but not just any kind of help. Even in your own life, when you require assistance, you don't need just any kind. You need the *right* help.

If you were swimming in a pool or lake and suddenly began to drown, would you want someone who was intoxicated to help you? No. You're yelling "Help!" and the person who comes to your rescue is so drunk he can barely walk, see or think. It's help, but not the right kind.

You need someone who is sober, sharp and alert — someone who knows how to save your life. So it is with the church.

All men and women of God who have been called to any of the five-fold offices of apostle, prophet, evangelist, pastor or teacher need assistance. But if they settle for just *any* help, they will be inviting problems that will eventually bring defeat and destruction. The problem with many local churches is that they've settled for *inebriated* help.

The church needs help from people who are faithful, committed, loyal and obedient. It requires help from people with certain qualities, characteristics, personalities, attitudes and mind sets. Most of all, it needs people who have a personal relationship with Christ and understand what it means to be anointed for service.

As our church grew, people were coming from all walks of life, backgrounds and denominations — each with his or her own understanding of what it meant to be involved in the church.

Some thought they could show up whenever they wanted to. They felt if they had a reasonable excuse to be absent from a meeting, the leaders would understand. Others wanted a title, yet were not prepared to work.

That's not what help is all about.

As I once told my congregation, "Some people just want their diapers changed. They say they want to be helpers, but they act like babies and only want attention."

When you say, "I'm ready to help," you must also say that you are prepared to grow up and take responsibility for leadership — that you can be counted upon.

No more diaper changing!

So that people would better understand our heart for this vital area of service, we began special classes on the Ministry of Helps. The classes are designed to give laymen a thorough understanding of the heart and mission of our ministry. They also help to ensure us of getting the right kind of help. The Bible says, "My people are destroyed for lack of knowledge" (Hosea 4:6).

As a direct result of individuals coming under the teaching you are about to read, our ministry has been strengthened and whenever I've taught this, churches and lives have been changed. May the same be true for you as you discover in the pages ahead what I believe God considers to be the right kind of help.

2

HELP THAT KNOWS THE VOICE OF GOD

The first requirement for getting involved in the Ministry of Helps is: *You must know the voice of God.*

Let me say it as clearly and as strongly as I can. If you don't know God's voice, you don't belong in any area of ministry — particularly leadership.

I say that in love because as a born again believer, I am convinced you can develop a relationship with the Lord that will make it possible for you to know His voice and His leading.

Several years ago, a friend of ours was a door greeter at a church in Tulsa. As the praise team sang, she stood in the foyer greeting the people. When no one was entering, she would join in singing, praising God and worshiping.

As she was singing, praising and worshiping, a woman on a walker entered and God spoke to our friend and said, "See that woman? Take that walker out of her hand and dance with her until I tell you to stop."

She immediately walked over and took the walker out of the woman's hand, took her by the hands and began to dance and dance and dance, until on the inside she heard, "STOP!" When she stopped, that woman was totally healed — completely whole.

Now, that's the right kind of help — the kind that knows the voice of God.

I remember going to Brother Kenneth Copeland's first East Coast Believer's Convention several years ago in the Charlotte Coliseum. I went to one minister's table after another — Hilton Sutton's, Jerry Savelle's and Charles Capps' — just browsing through books. I was just browsing because I had no money to buy anything. I was compiling a list of books I wanted so I could write in and purchase them later when I could afford them. But as I was browsing at Brother Capps' table, one of his workers came over to me and said, "Young man," and I responded, "Yes Ma'am?"

She said, "God just spoke to me and told me to let you have anything you want on this table."

Talk about happy! I was so happy and excited. It was thrilling to see God meet my spiritual need — right there on the spot — through someone who knew the voice of

God. The Lord knew where I was spiritually. He knew I was crying out, "God, I need these books!"

This was a woman sensitive enough to hear the voice of God. I'm not saying that those at the other tables weren't sensitive. I'm saying it's not hard to know the voice of God. This lady heard the voice of GOD and acted on what she heard!

Hearing from Heaven

Regardless of where you have been called to serve, it is essential that you hear from heaven.

> *Every usher* needs to know the voice of God.
> *Every door greeter* needs to know the voice of God.
> *Every nursery worker* needs to know the voice of God.
> *Every singer and musician* needs to know the voice of God.

Every person who works in any area of ministry should know the voice of God.

Why should people have to wait until the pastor calls a prayer line to receive a miracle? They ought to be healed when they are shaking the hand of an usher. They should receive something special from God when a greeter says "Good morning."

A tiny baby with a fever should be healed when the mother places the child in the loving arms of a nursery worker who has been walking and talking with the Lord.

You may ask, "Pastor Gool, why doesn't it happen that way?" The reason is simple:

Most well-meaning Christians don't give the work of the church the priority it deserves.

On Saturday, they rush to the malls, stop at their favorite restaurants and make it home in time to watch "something important" on television. Then their eyelids get heavy and they fall asleep — too exhausted to think about the ministry they are committed to the next day and too tired to pray.

When you take the Ministry of Helps seriously, you will find time to seek the face of God during the week — and especially on Saturday night.

You will get alone with the Lord and say:

- "Tomorrow, I'm going to be greeting people and I want Your anointing to flow through me!"
- "In the morning, I'll be working in the nursery and I want every child to sense Your presence."

- ■ "Tomorrow, I'm going to be the first person some see when they drive into the parking lot. Lord, cause them to see Jesus in me when I'm directing traffic."
- ■ "Lord, I've been asked to sing tomorrow. Let your anointing flow out of me. Let them sense your presence."

Every helper needs to know the voice of God to be a *supernatural* helper. For example, an usher who is spiritually sensitive can know exactly where to seat visitors. The voice of God may suddenly say: "The persons you're seating are witches and warlocks who have been sent on an assignment to disrupt the service. Seat them in the back and keep an eye on them. If they get up, you get up."

The usher may have been planning to take them to the front, but because he knows the voice of God, he is able to abort the plan before it ever gets started.

The spirit of God might speak to another usher telling him to "Take this person all the way to the front because they need to be very close to the anointing."

If the usher hears and obeys the voice of God it will make a difference in the individuals's life and the usher has been the right kind of help. On the other hand, let's say the usher, following the Spirit of God, proceeds to the section where the first five rows have been designated for counselors, ushers, musicians and others in the Ministry of Helps.

When he gets to that section, he finds that all of the front seats are already occupied. He explains to a counselor, "The Spirit of God told me to seat this person right here."

If the response he gets is, "Huh! This is *my* seat! You know I always sit here!" — then, that counselor is the wrong kind of help. The right kind of help would be quick to say, "Sure, I'll move and I agree with you that God is going to do something special in his life today."

We must have confidence in each other's ability to hear the voice of God and strip ourselves of pride.

All praise singers, especially praise and choir leaders, need to know the voice of God. Leaders who hear from God will know exactly what song to choose and will be ready to change plans at the leading of the Holy Spirit. Everything rehearsed may not be for the public worship service.

I remember when we were having one of our church dedication services, and there was a change in the flow of the service. I could sense it in my spirit.

It was now time for my singers to render a selection before the guest speaker came. When they began singing, the song wasn't with the flow of God. I jumped up, took the microphone and interrupted. I told them they had missed God and I gave the leader about a minute to get in tune with the spiritual flow of the service.

In about thirty seconds he said, "I've got it," and they began to minister a song that enhanced what God had started. Now that's the right kind of help.

25

You might say, "How embarrassing! I'd quit that praise team if that were me." Obviously you're the wrong kind of help.

To be the *right* kind of help you must know the voice of God. That will only happen when you spend time with Him. When you know His voice you can be transformed from an ordinary helper into an *extra*ordinary one. Instead of being a natural worker, you'll be *super*natural.

Where to Start

Knowing God's voice is not some perplexing, mysterious process. It simply takes spending time in His presence.

> *Turn off the television. Get off the phone. Unplug the computer. Begin praising and worshiping God and communing with Him in a heavenly language. Read and meditate on His Word.*

If you simply read His Word you will begin to hear His voice because God speaks through His Word. You'll soon know what God *will* and *will not* do, and you can find guidance and direction.

His ways are not hidden or obscure. Jesus said, "I am

the light of the world: he that followeth me shall not walk in darkness" (John 8:12).

The more time you spend in the Word of God, the easier it will be to discern His voice. The Bible says in Hebrews 4:12, "The word of God is quick, and powerful, and sharper than any two-edged sword, piercing even to the dividing asunder of soul and spirit, and of the joints and marrow, and is a discerner of the thoughts and intents of the heart."

The Word will make a distinction between your emotions, mind and spirit. We can know when God is speaking to us.

Likewise, the Lord expects you to hear His voice. Jesus declared, "My sheep hear my voice, and I know them, and they follow me" (John 10:27).

Before Christ ascended to heaven, He said, "It is expedient for you that I go away: for if I go not away, the Comforter will not come unto you; but if I depart, I will send him unto you" (John 16:7). And He added, "When he, the Spirit of truth, is come, he will guide you into all truth: for he shall not speak of himself; but whatsoever he shall hear, that shall he speak: and he will show you things to come" (John 16:13).

One of the reasons the Holy Spirit was sent was to speak to us concerning the things of God.

Are you committed to knowing the voice of God? Well you *can* and you'll find it's not just for the church. You need it for your very existence and well being.

I am convinced that knowing His voice helps us in the area of divine protection. Don't ignore His still small voice that may whisper, "Just sit at this traffic light another ten seconds. Don't take off right now." He could be protecting you from a car that will be zooming by within five seconds — running the red light.

The Lord will tell you where to look for a job, because He knows who's hiring before it is announced in the "Help Wanted" section of the newspaper.

He can show you how to be successful. "I am the Lord thy God which teacheth thee to profit" (Isaiah 48:17). The Holy Spirit will lead you in investing your money and even tell you who should be your partners in business.

Every aspect of your life should be directed by the Lord. That's why it is vital that you know His voice.

Let me bring some clarity here. God isn't going to tell you when to go to the restroom. You should know that instinctively. He isn't going to tell you when to go to work. If you're employed, you should already know your schedule. We are to go about our daily affairs, doing what we're supposed to do. However, we should always be ready to hear from headquarters and obey Him.

It's like a police officer. He goes about his job, doing

what he's supposed to do, but at anytime his superior calls on the police radio, he alters his plans and obeys the new assignment.

So it is with the Christian. God isn't going to tell you every little thing to do. Don't get spooky in relating to God or people.

Time for a Change?

It is only when you are serving the Lord, praying for the ministry and being sensitive to His Spirit that you will be able to act upon His leading.

When you know the voice of God, you should be quick to obey, even when He tells you to end your tenure in a particular area of ministry.

One time a member of our congregation came to me and said, "Pastor, I just sense in my heart that my time is running out in the area of service where I've been working. I feel God is getting me ready to be involved in some other ministry in the church."

I replied, "You're right. I've been meaning to get with you about that because it has been on my heart, too."

A church can be dynamic, changing and growing when it is filled with people who realize that their personal assignment is not of their choosing, but God's. You are not in one role forever unless the Lord says so.

At any moment He can say, "Your time as an usher is over. I need your talents somewhere else" — as a counselor, a singer, a nursery worker or on the broadcast crew.

29

Learn to listen to the Lord and flow with the direction He gives. Remember, His ways are always higher than ours.

There are many in the church, however, who do not feel ready to be helpers. They know there are adjustments they must first make in their lives.

Let me give you this advice: Don't wait too long to make the necessary changes. Begin by totally yielding to the Lord and let Him know you are ready to receive what He has to say. God doesn't want you to warm the pew forever.

The Holy Spirit did not draw you to the body of Christ to fold your arms and do nothing.

You are gifted and talented. Even though you may have to sit under ministry for a length of time and have some imperfections purged from your life, God is eventually going to tell you it's time to put your hand to the plow.

Are you ready to enter His service? It begins with knowing the voice of God.

3

HELP THAT SERVES AS UNTO THE LORD

In my years as a pastor I have watched in amazement at the variety of reasons people want to serve the church.

- They want to impress the minister.
- They want to be seen as being active in the church.
- They want to be elevated in the eyes of other members.
- They want to get close to the pastor or the pastor's wife.
- They want to please their spouses or be good examples to their children.
- They want to brag to their relatives and friends.

- They want to pay "penance" for their past misdeeds.
- They serve out of tradition.

If you are involved in ministry for any of these reasons you are missing the mark. God expects you to serve with only one motive: "And whatsoever ye do, do it heartily, as to the Lord, and not unto men" (Colossians 3:23).

The church doesn't require help from people who need their egos boosted or want to be praised from the pulpit. Their contributions to the ministry will bring diminishing returns.

My heart yearns for people to become involved who truly love God and desire to present their time and talents to Him and Him alone.

Stop looking for your pastor to constantly pat you on the back, saying, "Oh, I really appreciate you, brother. We couldn't live without you in this church."

Yes, I believe in proper commendation, but it certainly isn't needed week after week.

Those involved in the Ministry of Helps should be serving God, not the pastor.

Exposed Motives

The true reasons for your actions will always surface. When you are not serving as unto the Lord, it will surely be revealed.

I've known people who began staying away from church and holding back their tithes simply because they felt they weren't receiving the applause they deserved. Again, I must ask, "Who are they serving?"

> **God is always looking at your heart. You may attempt to deceive those around you, but the Lord knows what is on the inside.**

In his epistle, James warned the people about wrong motives, saying, "Ye ask, and receive not, because ye ask amiss, that ye may consume it upon your lusts" (James 4:3).

How much better it is to serve God because you are called, motivated and inspired by the Holy Spirit! Even if the preacher *never* tells you how well you are doing, you keep right on serving.

What a thrill it is for me to hear people say, "I'm so glad to be an usher for the Lord." Or, "I'm blessed to be serving Jesus in the children's ministry."

They are the ones who work with the attitude, "If the

pastor never pats me on the back, looks in my direction or hands me a plaque, it doesn't matter. I'll keep on serving because I am doing this for the Lord."

It is almost always these types of individuals who receive commendation. They don't seek it, yet it comes. Why? It comes because their hearts are right and they are of such obvious value to the church.

Here's a quick test to let you know whether your service is for God or man. *If the words or decisions of the pastor anger you, and you stop serving in the church or giving your tithes and offerings, you are not serving God.*

When your heart is right, you will perform your ministry with gladness and joy, regardless of any offenses that come your way to dissuade and distract you.

Pay Day is Coming

There is a distinct difference between working a job and working in the helps ministry. You are paid for a job but as a helper you look unto Jesus for your reward. You serve Him out of love, not for earthly payment.

Some people, however, don't seem to know the difference. When they are in a secular occupation they receive a paycheck, so when they serve in the church they expect to be paid.

I've encountered individuals who say they are working for the Lord, but in reality they are looking for compensation. They think, "I'm going to get involved, but what do I get out of it? I'll be an usher or a nursery worker so I can get a free tape."

They should say, "I don't need anything. I'm doing this because I love God and I love this ministry."

When you're looking for payment from man, you are not serving with the right motives. As a result, you will be inconsistent in your duties — one week committed and the next week uncommitted; sometimes enthusiastic and at other times unmotivated; sometimes faithful and other times unreliable. You will behave based on your emotions rather than your calling.

Now for the good news!

There is a reward — a great reward — for those who serve because of their love for the Lord.

Earlier we shared the admonition of the Apostle Paul: "And whatsoever ye do, do it heartily, as to the Lord, and not unto men" (Colossians 3:23). But listen to what he wrote in the very next verse. "Knowing that of the Lord ye shall receive the reward of the inheritance: for ye serve the Lord Christ" (v.24).

Pay day is coming!

35

You don't have to look to the pastor or to the church for compensation. God Himself is going to reward those who serve in the Ministry of Helps with the right spirit.

It's more than a hope or a wish. Paul says *"Knowing"* we shall receive the reward. That is not a minister's contract with you, but God's promise.

Don't try to bless yourself for serving the Lord. Let your Heavenly Father provide for you. It was God who placed you in His service, and He always takes good care of His children.

Excuses, Excuses!

It is easy to see when people are serving man rather than serving the Lord. I have seen members of my church immensely blessed by God as they've served Him instead of me and they have kept their hearts and motives pure — never looking for compensation through free food, tapes, special favors or even money. It is one thing for the pastor to give or offer these things but the helper should never ask for or demand them.

I know of music directors who go from church to church, playing two weeks here and two weeks there, just for money. Yet they rehearse only once a week and feel they must be paid.

There are people who do menial jobs or only donate a couple of hours of their time to the church but are looking for some form of compensation. What happened to just plain old "serving Jesus" and "loving God" service?

Another way you can tell when people are serving man rather than the Lord is by the number of excuses they make when they are supposed to be at meetings or when it is simply time to get involved in the church.

Over the years I've heard just about every excuse you can imagine.

> "Pastor, I really want to help, but we just had our first baby and I don't have the time!"
>
> "I would have been at the meeting, but we really needed to visit my aunt that night."
>
> "I couldn't make it last Sunday. My husband wasn't feeling well and I needed to stay at home with him."
>
> "My car has been acting up lately and I didn't think I should be driving."

Once, Jesus said to a man, "Follow me," and he replied, "Lord, suffer me first to go and bury my father" (Luke 9:59). Another said, "Lord, I will follow thee; but let me first go bid them farewell, which are at home at my house" (v.61).

The Lord replied, "No man, having put his hand to the plow, and looking back, is fit for the kingdom of God" (Luke 9:62).

Later, Jesus told the story of a man who invited many people to a supper he had prepared. He sent his servant to say, "Come, for all things are now ready" (Luke 14:17).

Instead of accepting the invitation, they all began to make excuses. The first said, "I have bought a piece of ground, and I must needs go and see it" (v.18). Another commented, "I bought five yoke of oxen, and I go to prove them: I pray thee have me excused. And another said, I have married a wife, and therefore I cannot come" (vv.19-20).

Do you remember the rest of the story? When the master heard the news he became angry and said to his servant, "Go out quickly into the streets and lanes of the city, and bring in hither the poor, and the maimed, and the halt, and the blind" (v.21).

When you are serving man, you will think of any reason why you can't be at the men's fellowship breakfast, why you can't attend the counselors' meeting or why you can't be at a special service.

However, when you are truly serving as unto the Lord your excuses will disappear. No longer will you say, "I know there's a meeting, but . . ." or "I really want to help, *but* . . ." You will be at your post at every opportunity because you couldn't possibly let Him down.

If you are going to get involved in ministry, accept the task with all of your heart, your soul, your mind and your strength. You are doing it for the Lord.

What's Your Priority?

God's work must become a priority.

When an ushers' meeting is called, every usher should be present. When the counselors have a session, every counselor should be there. Why? Because they are serving as unto the Lord.

Don't fit the work of God into your schedule; build your schedule around the work of the Lord.

Christ must come first — over recreation, over movies, over socializing; yes, and even over your parents or relatives when they come into town unexpectedly. You should greet them; tell them to make themselves at home and inform them that you'll be back in a few hours. Tell them you have to go to church for a meeting, an activity or a service. What an example of commitment and faithfulness that would be!

Of course there can be an emergency in your life that can keep you from attending or serving. God understands and so do pastors. However, it must be the exception, not the rule.

Get Ready to Serve

Sooner or later there will be a tugging in your heart saying, "I want you to get involved in this." We are *all* called to fulfil the Great Commission outside the doors of the church, but once God places you in a ministry, He expects you to serve eventually. When that moment arrives, remember you are not serving the congregation or its leadership, but God.

If you are planning to serve in the helps ministry, pray first, and commit your service to the Lord. If you're already involved in the helps ministry, it's time to evaluate and reassess why you are serving.

The Word tells us, "Whatsoever ye do, do all to the glory of God" (1 Corinthians 10:31).

Practice humility in every aspect of your work for Him. Jesus declared: "Whosoever shall exalt himself shall be abased; and he that shall humble himself shall be exalted" (Matthew 23:12).

Pray earnestly about your personal place of ministry. Let the Holy Spirit guide you in your decision.

That's important because when you are dedicated to working for the Lord, you won't be tempted to give up when the going gets tough. Instead of being part of the problem, you will be part of the solution.

What kind of help is needed?

- Help that knows the voice of God.
- Help that serves as unto the Lord.

I encourage you to pray, "Father, search my heart. I want my motives to be right. My only desire is to serve and worship You." In Jesus' name, Amen.

4

HELP THAT IS FAITHFUL

The routine seldom changed. I swept the floors, knocked on doors, set up chairs, took down chairs and tutored children — service after service, week after week.

This pattern continued as I gladly served a pastor in Tulsa, Oklahoma, while attending school at Oral Roberts University. I was so excited about serving in the ministry. I never became discouraged because I had made a commitment to the Lord and to that pastor to be faithful. Eventually, I was allowed to preach twice a month.

After graduation, and in the midst of serving the pastor, God opened doors for me to become the pastor of a small country church in Cushing, Oklahoma. Every weekend I drove 120 miles round trip to preach to 16 people. One thing was certain. Sunday after Sunday that small congregation could count on my being there. Because of my commitment to God and to them, I was faithful. In fact, I would drive the same distance during the week to visit members who were hospitalized. Some of my friends and colleagues thought I was crazy for driving that distance to pastor a church so small.

Pastors Need Help

What kind of help do pastors need? Help from people who are faithful.

Certainly there are people a pastor can count on like the rising of the sun. However, there are others who come when they want to, leave when they please and give financially when they feel like it.

Then, there are others who wake up pondering over where the Holy Spirit is leading them to go to church each Sunday. And they hop from ministry to ministry.

God requires that people be faithful to one ministry. Faithfulness is not only the backbone of a strong church, it is the foundation of a strong Christian.

The Lord wants you to grow and blossom where you are planted until He instructs you to go in a different direction.

What does it mean to be faithful? It means we are dependable, reliable and loyal. Another definition of *faithful* is an obligation to defend and support; firmly adhering to duty.

Every Christian expects God to be faithful. Shouldn't He have the right to expect the same from us?

When we read the Word it is obvious that the Lord blessed great leaders because they were steadfast and reliable. They were faithful.

For at least twenty years, Elisha served Elijah. That's a long time carrying a man's coat and bringing him water.

Even though these two men were not related, they developed a father-son bond. Just before Elijah was taken to heaven in a whirlwind, Elisha cried, "My father, my father" (2 Kings 2:12).

It was also that relationship that prompted Elijah to ask his beloved friend, "Ask what I shall do for thee, before I be taken away from thee. And Elisha said, I pray thee, let a double portion of thy spirit be upon me" (2 Kings 2:9).

In those days, a first born son received a double portion of the inheritance. Elisha's faithfulness brought him into a father-son relationship with Elijah, and a double portion of Elijah's anointing came upon him.

Father to Son

During the three-and-a-half year ministry of Jesus on earth, He was faithful to fulfill the work of His Father. "For I came down from heaven, not to do mine own will, but the will of him that sent me" (John 6:38).

What did God say about the ministry of Christ? He spoke from heaven and declared, "This is my beloved Son, in whom I am well pleased; hear ye him" (Matthew 17:5).

God would not have uttered those words if Christ was not fulfilling His purpose.

The writer of Hebrews asks us to consider Jesus, "Who was faithful to him that appointed him, as also Moses was faithful in all his house" (Hebrews 3:2).

Christ is faithful "as a son over his own house; whose house are we, if we hold fast the confidence and the rejoicing of the hope firm unto the end" (v.6).

He earned the trust of His heavenly Father during His earthly ministry, and we can continue to rely on Him as He is faithful over His own house (the body of Christ).

- He is faithful and just to forgive us of our sins and to cleanse us from all unrighteousness. Hallelujah!
- He is faithful to back up His Word. Praise God!
- He is faithful to provide the harvest for what you sow, "good measure, pressed down,

shaken together and running over." Thank you Jesus!
- He is faithful to bring healing and deliverance. Glory! Glory!

Everything we own is the result of God keeping His promises. He's faithful. As followers of Christ, our lives must be patterned after His.

Throwing Darts

How would you respond if you knew someone was talking negatively about you during every meal — discussing you before they went to bed? That is what many believers are doing relative to their pastors.

I don't mind if the world attacks me — in fact, I'd be disappointed if they didn't. What bothers me immensely, however, is when a member of the body of Christ becomes unfaithful and lashes out against me. It's okay for the neighbor's dog to try and bite me, but not my own.

I can understand the unsaved throwing darts. I can even comprehend the criticism of someone from another doctrine or faith. However, it is not God's will for church members to be engaged in a battle with each other, or with the person the Lord has chosen to lead them.

When we were building our multi-purpose building, it was a pay-as-we-go project. There were nay-sayers who would drive by and comment, "They'll never finish that!"

Even a handful of church members said, "I'm not sure if we're going to make it" — and they left the church.

It's been said that the first thing off a sinking ship are the rats. But we weren't sinking. Some people, however, came to that mistaken conclusion because of the slow construction schedule. I wonder what they think now that the building is completed and serving over-capacity crowds? God is faithful.

> *When you know God has sent you to a church, He expects you to remain steadfast when the waters are calm and when they are rough. The ministry deserves your faithful support.*

Captains of Conflict

Here is an important word of caution. Don't allow a group of dissenters to appoint you as their captain.

There are people who become irritated over some issue in the church and begin to whisper to anyone who will listen, "I don't like what is going on around here."

They delight in starting a negative "undercurrent."

Most times their target is the pastor. They say, "I don't like what he's preaching. I disagree with what he's teaching. I'm against the decisions he is making."

Next, they're on the phone trying to build a case for

their opinions. They congregate on the parking lot after service to condemn the church and back-stab the pastor. Then, they invite people to their homes to talk even more about their dissatisfaction.

Finally, they ask, "Why don't you represent us and go to the pastor?"

Don't ever be a part of anything like this and never let anyone make you a captain. Captains die premature deaths.

Before falling into the trap of becoming a spokesperson for someone else's crusade, think about what happened when the children of Israel began to murmur against Moses and appointed a captain to lead their dissention.

They complained, "And wherefore hath the Lord brought us unto this land, to fall by the sword, that our wives and our children should be a prey? Were it not better for us to return into Egypt? And they said one to another, Let us make a captain, and let us return into Egypt" (Numbers 14:3-4).

Why do I warn you about allowing those filled with strife to make you their spokesperson? Because captains die! And by the way, so do those who follow them.

A man by the name of Korah lead a group of 250 famous men in the congregation to challenge Moses' spiritual leadership. A showdown came at the Tent of Meeting and God brought instant judgement on the rebels.

Those who came against Moses met a bizarre and

untimely death. "The earth opened her mouth, and swallowed them up, and their houses, and all the men that appertained unto Korah, and all their goods" (Numbers 16:32). Entire families died premature deaths because they fought against the man of God.

When I was in the CME church, a group of members began coming against me. They claimed that my sermons weren't Methodist and that they weren't from the Bible. Some of them called or wrote the bishop and the elder to complain about me.

Because I never attempted to retaliate, but continued to walk in love with them all, I saw the hand of God move mightily on my behalf. As He began to promote me more and more, my wife and I began to notice hardships coming to each of those people. That's because the Word warns: "Touch not mine anointed, and do my prophets no harm" (Psalms 105:15).

When you can't be faithful to your church and pastor, you should find another church because you'll begin to murmur and complain. It's when you can't be loyal, dependable and reliable, and you don't have the obligation to defend and support the church that you become extremely judgmental of every little thing. It is then that you're on dangerous ground. Often people bring tumors and cancers on themselves by coming against men and women of God.

If you don't like what's going on in your church to the extent that you can't be faithful, you ought to do one of three things. Set up an appointment with your pastor to talk it out; pray and ask God to help you support the ministry; or leave and find another church.

The Standard

Don't expect God to give you your own ministry until you first prove yourself by blessing *another* person's ministry or vision. He never opens new doors until you become dedicated and committed to where you've been placed.

Some people are faithful, but to the wrong things.

It's amazing how loyal a Christian can be to a certain television program. They will never miss it! If the program is scheduled every Thursday night, the pastor had better not expect them to be in church that evening. No way! "That's my television night."

Should church attendance drop dramatically on Super Bowl Sunday night? Of course not. Unfortunately, it does.

If you want to understand what commitment really is, listen to the Word: "If ye then be risen with Christ, seek those things which are above, where Christ sitteth on the right hand of God. Set your affection on things above, not on things on the earth" (Colossians 3:1-2).

People demand faithful leadership, but set lower standards for themselves.

What would you think if your pastor arrived 45 minutes late for the Sunday morning service and told the congregation, "I just felt like sleeping in this morning"?

Or, "There was a good movie on television last night and I didn't get to bed until late." How about, "I had guests over last night and we stayed up late laughing and having a good time." Or, "I just didn't feel good this morning!"

Most Christians would leave the church if their pastor gave those excuses. They'd say, "What kind of pastor is that? He should be here when no one else is. He should be on time."

Yet that's exactly what members do. They come late with all kinds of excuses, or simply don't come at all.

Some pastors ought to put a sign on their doors on Sunday morning saying, "Closed because of unfaithful members."

It's amazing how members expect faithfulness from their pastors, but pastors can't expect it from them. There ought to be reciprocity. Members expect pastors to be at every service, and on time. They should apply that same attitude to themselves.

When you declare that you are going to accept an area of responsibility in the church, everything else must revolve around that decision.

Let's say you receive a phone call from your mother in Oregon. She tells you she's flying in to see you next weekend and that her plane will arrive just before noon on Sunday.

How will you respond?

Hopefully, you'll say, "I'm thrilled you're coming Mom, but as you know, I am an usher at church so I will have to arrange for someone else to pick you up." And you might add, "Mother, because you raised me to be committed to the church, I will not be home until after I finish my duties."

It's that kind of commitment the Lord blesses. Remember, it's "a faithful man that abounds with blessings."

Some people wonder why they are not promoted at secular jobs. Why should they be when they are the last to arrive and the first to go home? That's no way to display commitment. Nor will it cause your boss to have confidence in you.

The Bible says, "Confidence in an unfaithful man in time of trouble is like a broken tooth, and a foot out of joint" (Proverbs 25:19). It can really hurt! And that's one reason many churches are experiencing pain and are ineffective. A man with a broken foot can't move quickly or do much at all. This gives us a graphic picture of the state of many churches. It's time for a change.

Change Starts Today

The lessons I learned during my years in Oklahoma have never left me. I discovered what Jesus meant when He declared, "He that is faithful in that which is least is faithful also in much: and he that is unjust in the least is unjust also in much" (Luke 16:10).

I've heard people say, "When God blesses me with more, I'll be able to start giving."

According to the Bible, that's a lie.

> ## *If you are not faithful with what you have today — whether it is your time or your tithe — it is highly unlikely that your acquiring more will cause you to change.*

In other words, if you are stingy with a few assets now, you'll be stingy with much more later. Faithfulness starts today.

Christ continued, "If therefore ye have not been faithful in the unrighteous mammon, who will commit to your trust the true riches?" (v.11).

Will God trust you? I think not. "If ye have not been faithful in that which is another man's, who shall give you that which is your own?" (v. 12).

There is a great message in those words. If you want to receive God's blessing you must be willing to commit to someone else's vision and to become devoted to that which is not your own — not with a stepping-stone mentality, but with true commitment, loyalty and dedication.

When I served that pastor in Oklahoma, it wasn't with

the attitude, "I wonder how long I've got to do this." Or, "I'm just going to learn what I can because I'm not staying here long."

No. It was service as unto the Lord, giving my all, without thinking about myself or my future.

It is only after willingly and faithfully committing to the vision of another that God will deem you ready for a ministry of your own.

Faithfulness Starts Today

Faithfulness is required at *every* level of ministry. God has called the pastor to lead and He has chosen you to serve.

When your pastor shares his vision and announces a new building program, you should be ready to respond, "Go for it, pastor. I'm with you all the way!"

Then, your words should be followed by actions. When financial commitments are required, you will respond. When volunteers are needed during construction, you will be there.

You will support the vision prayerfully, physically, financially and verbally.

Verbal support is an area of faithfulness that is sometimes overlooked. Remember, a part of the definition of faithfulness is an obligation to defend and support.

Don't be in the presence of people who talk about your pastor or church without defending it. It's your obligation to stand up for the church in which God has placed you. Let me give you an example.

A member of my church was eating at a restaurant when he heard some people behind him lambasting a church and its pastor. The more they talked, he realized it was *his* church and *his* pastor.

When these people got up to pay the cashier, he followed them. After they paid, he said, "Excuse me, weren't you talking about a church at your table?"

They answered, "Yes, we were."

He continued, "Have you ever been to that church? Have you ever talked with the pastor?" They responded, "No, we haven't."

The member said to them, "Well, that's my church and I don't appreciate your talking against my church and my pastor without ever having been there. Please don't do that again."

Stunned, they replied, "Okay," and quickly left the restaurant.

Now that's faithfulness. I'm not saying you have to go that far, but you should always be ready to speak up for your church and pastor. You should never belong to a church that you don't hold in high esteem.

Where it Begins

If we do our part, God does His. It begins with salvation. God honors John 1:12: "But as many as received him, to them gave he power to become the sons of

God, even to them that believe on his name." After receiving Christ, if we sin, He is faithful to I John 1:9 which says, "If we confess our sins, he is faithful and just to forgive us our sins, and to cleanse us from all unrighteousness."

From that moment forward, God expects you to remain steadfast in His love and service. Jesus said, "But he that shall endure unto the end, the same shall be saved" (Matthew 24:13).

What kind of help is needed in ministry?

- Help that knows the voice of God.
- Help that serves as unto the Lord.
- Help that is faithful.

When God plants you in a church, the cry of your heart should be, "Lord, you can count on me to serve you here." It is a commitment that must continue until God clearly releases you from that place of service.

Remember, the church must never rely on superficial, temporary assistance. It requires loyal, faithful help.

Is that what you are offering?

5

HELP THAT IS COMMITTED TO EXCELLENCE

When I was growing up in Detroit my mom and dad had a special note board in our house. On it was tacked a piece of paper with these words: "Chores for Today."

Every afternoon, when I came home from school, that's the first place I looked. My instructions would be posted there.

"Mow the grass."

"Empty the garbage."

"Mop the kitchen floor."

Mopping the floor actually meant getting down on my

hands and knees with a pail of soapy water and scrubbing it by hand. Often, I'd try to rush through the task and would think, "Well, if I don't really clean that corner, nobody's going to see it."

Like most children, I'd speed through the work, anxious to yell, "I'm finished."

Then, a few minutes later, my mother would walk into the kitchen and turn on the light. I can still hear her voice: "Robyn, come back in here! Get your bucket. You're going to have to do it all over again because you missed that corner."

The very corner I didn't think she would see, would be the first place mom looked.

I made the same mistake in cutting the grass. In my haste, I'd miss a spot and my dad would say, "Son, get the lawn mower back out. Look at that area you didn't mow."

It didn't take too long for me to learn a valuable lesson:

If you're going to do it, do it right the first time!

No Short Cuts

Today, when I observe how casually some people treat their ministry assignment, I wonder, "Don't they know they serve a God of excellence?"

The Lord takes no short cuts. He is a God of quality

and He does it right the first time!

You can see it from cover to cover in your Bible that when the Creator does something, it is never done carelessly or haphazardly. He demands quality and perfection.

- At creation, "God saw everything that he had made, and, behold, it was very good" (Genesis 1:31).
- Noah was given precise instructions on how to design and construct the best possible ark (Genesis 6:15-16).
- The Lord delivered the children of Israel to a bountiful land "flowing with milk and honey" (Exodus 3:8).
- Only the finest craftsmen were used to build Solomon's temple in Jerusalem (1 Kings 7:14).
- Heaven is a place of unspeakable beauty (Revelation 4:3-6).

The word excellence is derived from the word *excel,* which means to be superior, majestic, magnificent; to surpass or exceed.

All of those terms can be applied to our omnipotent God — "His mighty acts, and the glorious majesty of his kingdom" (Psalms 145:12).

The people made the same observation of Jesus. "He hath done all things well" (Mark 7:37).

At the marriage feast at Cana in Galilee, when Christ

turned water into wine, the governor of the feast ex-claimed, "You have saved the best till now" (John 2:10).

Everything Jesus accomplished on earth was beyond the ordinary and always much more than expected. He does "exceeding abundantly above all that we ask or think" (Ephesians 3:20).

Five Principles of Excellence

How can we rise to a level of excellence that God expects? Here are five principles to follow.

One: Realize that you were created to walk in excellence.

It is important to understand that we are not an accident of nature. Scripture tells us we were "fearfully and wonderfully made" (Psalms 139:14).

You were divinely designed by the Almighty and were placed on earth to be a reflection of Him. You were created "in the image of God" (Genesis 9:6).

What the Lord expects from you is not second class or mediocre, but *the best*. The Apostle Paul wrote, "For we are his workmanship, created in Christ Jesus unto good works, which God hath before ordained that we should walk in them." (Ephesians 2:10).

Some people believe that their being in the will of God excludes them from having to perform at their best. Somehow, they feel God's anointing on them to perform a particular task will more than make up for their slackness.

That's faulty thinking. The will of God must be performed at the highest possible level. The Word tells us to "stand perfect and complete in all the will of God" (Colossians 4:12), and that we are kings and priests — a royal priesthood. Kings demand the best and *expect* the best, both of themselves and others.

Not only that, but as His offspring and ambassadors, we must represent Him accurately.

> *People see the Lord based on our actions — what we do, what we say, our attitude and how we complete our assignments.*

Put your shoulders back and hold your head up high. You are a son or a daughter of the Most High God and He expects you to walk in excellence.

Two: Never settle for being "average."

It's been said that average is the top of the bottom and the bottom of the top. That's not where we want to live.

Only two percent of America's entire work force can work without supervision. Those in this motivated minority are self-starters who are filled with visions, dreams and goals.

What about the other 98 percent? They need direction — someone looking over their shoulders. Eighty-four percent sit back and do nothing and 14 percent will perform, but not without prodding.

If you are serious about serving God, you won't need someone constantly checking to see if you are keeping your commitment. You will not only fulfill your promise, but you will go beyond the call of duty.

My friend John Mason wrote a powerful book entitled *An Enemy Called Average.* In it he says, "Mediocrity is a region bounded on the north by compromise, on the south by indecision, on the east by past thinking and on the west by a lack of vision."

I am often puzzled as to why so many who call themselves Christians demonstrate such a slothful, lethargic attitude toward the work of the Kingdom.

They will write a bad check and place it in the offering plate. They'd never intentionally do that to their mortgage company! In many ways, some Christians have relegated the church to their lowest priority. It's generally the same people who are willing to settle for second best or average.

I pray you never fall into that camp.

When members of a congregation make a decision to go beyond what is normal, phenomenal things start to happen. You can see it in the way the ushers walk, the way the counselors talk and the way the musicians play their instruments.

As a result, your church will no longer be an "average" church. It will take on an entirely new dimension and move to a higher level — spiritually, physically and materially.

However, that won't happen until a significant number in the congregation begin to say, "That's what I am praying for and I'm going to do my part."

Look at I Kings 10. "And when the Queen of Sheba heard of the fame of Solomon concerning the name of the Lord, she came to prove him with hard questions" (v.1).

"And when the queen of Sheba had seen all Solomon's wisdom and the house that he had built, and the meat of his table, and the sitting of his servants, and the attendance of his ministers, and their apparel, and his cupbearers, and his ascent by which he went up unto the house of the Lord; there was no more spirit in her. And she said to the king, It was a true report that I heard in mine own land of thy acts and of thy wisdom" (vv. 4-6).

Then, after she learned the truth of Solomon's great wisdom and riches, she said, "Howbeit I believed not the words, until I came, and my eyes had seen it: and, behold, the half was not told to me: thy wisdom and prosperity exceedeth the fame which I heard" (v.7).

Did you catch that? The Queen of Sheba lost her breath over the excellence she saw and then said that half its greatness had not been described to her. That's what people ought to say when visiting your church.

Everybody, from the custodian to the pastor, should be committed to a walk of excellence.

> *Both excellence and mediocrity*
> *are contagious. Churches rise and fall*
> *based on what is in the hearts of those*
> *who lead and those who help.*

Just being "good" at your task is not enough. God wants you to grow, develop and climb to a height you have never before reached. Every singer should aspire to be a better singer. Every teacher should strive to be a superior teacher. Every individual involved in personal evangelism should pray to become more effective in leading people to Christ.

Just as mediocrity will rob you of the advancement and promotion God has in store for you, a spirit of excellence in ministry will cause you to reap astonishing benefits that will enhance your personal development.

Don't be ordinary. Learn a skill and perfect it in Jesus' Name.

Three: Always give God your best.

"Lord, I need your anointing. I want your financial blessings. Give me health for my physical body. Please Lord, I want your favor."

Heaven is bombarded with such personal requests. Yet, we fail to hear God saying, "I want your best, too. I covet your worship. I desire that you forgive. I am asking you to tithe and to get involved in the Ministry of Helps."

If you want God's finest, don't you believe He also wants yours? Why should you place demands on Him and not allow the Lord to place demands on you?

Pay close attention to the words of the Apostle Paul: "For it is God which worketh in you both to will and to do of his good pleasure" (Philippians 2:13).

The Lord is working in you so that you will represent Him in excellence. He doesn't want you to be a Christian in name only — but also in word and deed.

When you're walking in a spirit of excellence, you'll find it a lot easier to flow in the gifts of the Spirit, cast out devils, lay hands on the sick, lift the hands of your pastor, lead people to a saving knowledge of Christ and do all things well.

People should be able to look at you and say, "That's a Christian!"

What I am speaking of will not happen unless you are aspiring to serve the Lord with excellence.

Paul told the Philippians that before his conversion he had great credentials to be a religious leader. He was "Circumcised the eighth day, of the stock of Israel, of the tribe of Benjamin, an Hebrew of the Hebrews; as touching the law, a Pharisee; Concerning zeal, persecuting the church; touching the righteousness which is in the law, blameless" (Philippians 3:5-6).

Then Paul declared, "But what things were gain to me,

those I counted loss for Christ . . . for the excellency of the knowledge of Christ Jesus my Lord: for whom I have suffered the loss of all things, and do count them but dung, that I may win Christ" (vv.7-8).

He explained that it was "Not that I have already obtained all this, or have already been made perfect, but I press on to take hold of that for which Christ Jesus took hold of me" (v.12 NIV).

Paul was saying the things that he had accomplished were insignificant compared to the excellence in store for him through Christ.

Don't make the mistake of feeling you have "arrived" just because you can quote certain scriptures or move in a particular gift of the Spirit. There is more.

We must continue to strive to go from glory to glory.

Paul didn't just think about being the best, he put it into action. He declared: "Brethren, I count not myself to have apprehended: but this one thing I do, forgetting those things which are behind, and reaching forth unto those things which are before, I press toward the mark for the prize of the high calling of God in Christ Jesus" (vv. 13-14).

Regardless of the area of ministry in which you serve, press toward the highest mark. Fulfilling the call to serve takes more than aspiration. It requires perspiration.

Why settle for barely reaching a comfortable plateau. If you accelerate your effort, God will not only match it, He will promote you to higher realms. "And the Lord shall make thee the head, and not the tail; and thou shalt be above only, and thou shalt not be beneath" (Deuteronomy 28:13).

Four: Walking in excellence requires a decision.

Walking in excellence is a choice. You must come to the point where you say, "I refuse to live in mediocrity. I refuse to be complacent or inferior. From this moment, I will choose what is best."

It begins with a decision. We are where we are today because of the decisions we've made in the past.

Throughout the Bible there were mighty moves of God immediately after people made steadfast decisions. The rewards they reaped were based on their decisions.

- Moses stood in the gate of the camp, and asked, "Who is on the Lord's side? Let him come to me" (Exodus 32:26).
- Again, Moses asked for a decision: "I have set before you life and death, blessing and cursing: therefore choose life, that both thou and thy seed may live" (Deuteronomy 30:19).
- Joshua stood before the people and said,

"Choose you this day whom ye will serve . . . but for me and my house, we will serve the Lord" (Joshua 24:15).

- Jairus, a ruler of the synagogue, *decided* to go to Christ to ask Him to pray for his dying daughter. "He fell down at Jesus' feet, and besought him that he would come into his house" (Luke 8:41).
- The woman with the issue of blood *decided* to go to Jesus. She "Came behind him, and touched the border of his garment" and was immediately healed (Luke 8:44).

Nothing comes automatically. God says "if" you will meet certain conditions, here's how I will respond. For example, "If ye be willing and obedient, ye shall eat the good of the land" (Isaiah 1:19).

That's a decision only you can make. Are you willing? Are you obedient? Are you ready to commit to walk in excellence?

The choice is yours.

Five: Demonstrating excellence demands total commitment.

Being the best requires self-discipline, consistency and dedication to the task. Without those qualities you will be headed down a long, slippery slope.

The lazy person complains, "I wish I lived in a house

like that." Or, "God is really using them. I wish He would use me like that someday!"

They desire and covet promotion, yet aren't willing to pay the price for it. The Word says, "The soul of the sluggard desireth, and hath nothing: but the soul of the diligent shall be made fat" (Proverbs 13:4).

Laziness also leads to poverty. "He becometh poor that dealeth with a slack hand: but the hand of the diligent maketh rich" (Proverbs 10:4).

Who does God lift into areas of leadership? Those who are hard-working and industrious. "The hand of the diligent shall bear rule: but the slothful shall be under tribute" (Proverbs 12:24).

When you are conscientious, consistent and dependable, God will honor and promote you. Why? Because "He is a rewarder of them that diligently seek him" (Hebrews 11:6).

The Lord does not advance or elevate those who are lazy — in secular jobs or in the church.

We simply cannot take the risk of doing the work of Christ in a half-hearted, inconsistent, sloppy manner. Every believer, at every level, must commit himself to excellence.

The Holy Spirit will lead us, guide us and deal with all areas of our lives. There comes a time, however, when our action is required.

Are you ready to make a permanent commitment to diligence, persistence and excellence?

Demonstrate It!

God does not tell us to: "Lay down. Give up. Don't try to succeed!" Instead, He is working to lift us higher and add quality to our lives.

If you have made a decision to excel, let it show. Demonstrate it in your dress, your smile, your handshake, your work, your attitude and the words you speak.

Remember this: *Quality attracts quality.* If we expect to be true representatives of God's Kingdom, we must set examples. People never rise above what they don't see. If they can't visualize beyond their present circumstances, that is where they will remain.

Let God know that you are going to please Him in every assignment you are given and every project you undertake. Then demonstrate it.

What kind of help is needed?

- Help that knows the voice of God.
- Help that serves as unto the Lord.
- Help that is faithful.
- Help that is committed to excellence.

The writer of Hebrews prayed that God would "Make you perfect in every good work to do his will, working in you that which is wellpleasing in his sight" (Hebrews 13:21).

This should also be your prayer. Say, "Lord, from this moment forward, I commit myself to excellence. No matter what the task, I will not stop until the finished product deserves your stamp of approval."

Make a commitment to God, to your church and to yourself to do all things well.

6

HELP THAT HAS THE LEADER'S SPIRIT

If you are going to be an effective member of a church or ministry, you must share the same burden, the same vision and the same heart as that of your leader.

Earlier we recalled the story of how God asked Moses to appoint seventy elders to help bear the load of leadership as he led the children of Israel through the wilderness. Do you know what the paradox is? They were already supposed to be the helpers for Moses. Evidently they were not the kind of help that he needed.

The Lord gave Moses specific instructions. The elders

were to gather at the tabernacle, and they were to all stand together in unity.

Then, God made this promise. "I will come down and talk with thee there: and I will take of the spirit which is upon thee, and will put it upon them; and they shall bear the burden of the people with thee, that thou bear it not thyself alone" (Numbers 11:17).

God was telling Moses that in order to have the right kind of help, those chosen would need to have the spirit of their leader.

The Lord said, "I am going to take your spirit and place it upon the elders."

> *The kind of help that is desperately needed comes from people who have within them the spirit of their leader.*

When the seventy were gathered together for their first meeting in the tabernacle, God delivered on His promise. The Bible says, "The Lord came down in a cloud, and spake unto him, and took of the spirit that was upon him, and gave it unto the seventy elders" (Numbers 11:25).

What anointing did Moses have on him? It was the

Spirit of God.

When we say that you need to have the spirit of your pastor, we are talking about a portion of the anointing and a measure of the Spirit of God the Lord has placed upon his life.

The Outpouring

Don't overlook this important point. These seventy men were already leaders. They were elders *before* God called them out. However, they did not become the right kind of help to Moses until the spirit of the leader was transferred by God to them.

The elders not only received the heart and vision of Moses, there was also an immediate outpouring of *God's* Spirit.

The Bible states: "And it came to pass, that, when the spirit rested upon them, they prophesied, and did not cease" (Numbers 11:25).

This was something that had never happened before. When they were in unity with their spiritual leader, God began to speak through them with prophecy. There was a spiritual lifting — an elevation that took place, bringing them closer to the Lord. Suddenly, they tapped into the realm of the Spirit.

God is still giving the same message to the church. You will not become the kind of help your church needs until you take on your pastor's spirit.

It doesn't matter how much you love your pastor or how long you've been with him. You need his spirit in order to be the right kind of help.

You'll Know It!

A transformation will take place when the spirit of your pastor is yours.

- You will begin to see the ministry from a totally new perspective — more from the eye and the heart of your pastor.
- You will become aware that the vision he is carrying is resting on your shoulders as well.
- You will become more sensitive to the move of the Holy Spirit.

There are several people in our congregation who have told me: "Pastor, many times I know what you are going to preach before you even step in the pulpit."

One member said, "Before you ever made that announcement I told my family, 'Something is stirring inside the pastor. I just feel it in my spirit.'"

Others have shared how they often know when the gifts of the Spirit are about to begin to operate in a particular service.

75

Why are they able to respond in such a manner? They have tapped into my heart. There is a portion of my anointing from God in them.

As a pastor it is encouraging to know there are people who are committed to your leadership and linked to God's vision for your ministry.

United We Stand

When the church and the pastor are a spiritual team, Satan's best laid plans are blocked. For example, if a few trouble-makers attempt to cause strife, it can be immediately detected — not just by the pastor, but by a growing number of members who are united in spirit.

Since the pastor will not tolerate dissension and confusion, you won't either. You will say to those who are causing friction, "Let's pray about this. That's not the way we do things in this church."

- You will seek peace and harmony because that's what your pastor seeks.
- You will desire to grow spiritually, because that's what your leader desires.
- You will want to win your city to Christ because that is the heart of your pastor.

Without a strong core of men and women who are serving as God intends, a congregation can experience difficulties.

I've seen churches split and ministries disband because certain people have clenched their fists, hardened their hearts and refused to follow spiritual leadership.

How can you know if you *don't* have your pastor's spirit? You will resist his direction. You will disagree with his vision. You will sometimes become rigid and defensive in his presence.

That is not God's desire for His church, for the pastor, or for you.

Paul prayed "that ye stand fast in one spirit, with one mind striving together for the faith of the gospel" (Philippians 1:27).

Whose Vision?

The Lord didn't say, "Moses, gather seventy elders together because I want to put the spirit of just any man of God on them."

They were not about to receive the mantle of Abraham, the dream of Jacob, the insight of Joseph, the revelation of Joshua or the vision of Aaron.

The order God gave was not for another day or an earlier time. Moses was their leader and it was *his* spirit that was needed by the elders.

When the Lord places you in a church, He will prepare you to receive what He has planted within the mind and heart of your pastor — not that of a former minister, a popular evangelist, or a preacher in some other part of the country.

If the Lord wants you to have the spirit of Marilyn Hickey or Kenneth Hagin, he will move you to Colorado or Oklahoma to become involved in their ministries.

I have met many well-meaning Christians whose lives have become entwined in the teachings of a particular man or woman of God who resides in some distant city. The problem is that these Christians are not plugged into ministry in their local churches. They become like parasites — always taking in, but never giving. And most times, they begin to judge their pastors based on the ministers in distant cities. This certainly isn't the will of God.

The Lord's desire is that "ye be likeminded, having the same love, being of one accord, of one mind" (Philippians 2:2).

Closing the Door

It is often difficult for people to move to a new church or sit under the ministry of a newly elected pastor.

We have a tendency to cling to the past because we are creatures of habit and resist change. Often, we become so attached to a particular pastor that we won't consider allowing someone else to take his place in our heart.

In order to accept God's plan for building His church, we must learn to close certain chapters in our lives and open new ones.

Let me give you this word of advice:

Changing churches is much like changing clothes. You must take off the old and put on the new.

You might enjoy the singing, love the preaching and sense the anointing in your new house of worship. However, you think, "I know I belong here, but something doesn't feel right."

Friend, you *are* in the right place — you just haven't yet changed clothes! You've got to take off your Baptist, Methodist, Lutheran or Catholic garment and put on something new.

It may even be that you are moving from one charismatic or non-denominational church to another. The same admonition still applies.

Only when this has happened will you stop making comparisons and judging the present by the past. Accept the reality that God has given you a new pastor with a new vision for your life. Change clothes. Put on your new pastor's spirit.

One Accord

There is a tremendous difference between a violin solo and a great symphony orchestra — just as there is a noticeable contrast between a minister who is working alone and one who has a large number of people working in harmony with him.

> *When the same spirit is found in the pastor, the deacons, the elders, the ushers, the musicians and all those involved in the Ministry of Helps, the church becomes a mighty chorus.*

The Apostle Paul prayed that what we think and what we say will be in unity: "That ye may with one mind and one mouth glorify God, even the Father of our Lord Jesus Christ" (Romans 15:6).

Later, he told the believers at Corinth, "I beseech you, brethren, by the name of our Lord Jesus Christ, that ye all speak the same thing, and that there be no divisions among you; but that ye be perfectly joined together in the same mind and in the same judgment" (1 Corinthians 1:10).

The vision is not to baby-sit the saints, but to win the world for Christ.

When we work together, the task can be accomplished.

We can't become complacent. There are still those who are calling, "Come over into Macedonia, and help us" (Acts 16:9).

What kind of help does the church require?

- Help that knows the voice of God.
- Help that serves as unto the Lord.
- Help that is faithful.
- Help that is committed to excellence.
- Help that has the leader's spirit.

Ask your pastor to lay his or her hands on you for an impartation of his or her spirit. Just saying you have your pastor's spirit isn't enough.

Anointing is transferred in most cases by the laying on of hands. Declaring how much you love him or her isn't enough. You need your pastor to lay hands on you in faith, expecting God to deposit on you a portion of his anointing. It will be for you as it was for the elders. You'll "go up a notch in the realm of the spirit," and become the right kind of help.

7

GETTING INVOLVED

A s you read these pages, perhaps God is dealing with you concerning your role in the Ministry of Helps and being the right kind of help.

You may have even reached the point where you are ready to tell your pastor that God is urging you to become involved.

Every person in the helps ministry needs to fully understand what the Lord expects and what every pastor or minister desires of him.

Here are six additional things that will cause you to be most effective in the helps ministry.

One: Be aware that Satan may attack.

Your participation in ministry means that you have now gone beyond being an ordinary member of the church. No longer do you simply sit in a chair or a pew on Sunday morning, Sunday night and Wednesday night and then go home. You have become active and Satan doesn't like it.

Without realizing this and the responsibility that service brings, you may be in for serious problems. The higher you rise in ministry the more the devil will attack. But never forget that greater is He that is in you than he that is in the world! Satan is defeated and Jesus is Lord.

You are now becoming a threat to Satan. Therefore, he will say, "I'd better assign a demon to that person for a while!" He will aim his arrows and throw his fiery darts in a feverish attempt to get you to say, "I think it was better when I *wasn't* involved in ministry." But never forget you're more than a conqueror through Him that loves you, and that you've been given authority over all the power of the devil. Heaven is on your side!

Two: You should be in church every time the doors open.

What kind of win-loss record would a professional athletic team have if half of its members did not show up for games?

Not only would the team lose; but the absentees would be seriously fined or even fired from the team.

Ministries don't operate by remote control. Those who have been chosen to help are expected to be present when the doors of the church are open — rain or shine, hot or cold, headache or no headache.

What better place to be than in church if you have a headache. It's amazing to me that Christians stay home from church when they're not feeling well. God says we can lay hands on the sick and they shall recover. Go to the house of God and have hands laid on you! Get in the atmosphere of the anointing where the gifts of the Spirit can move. God is a healer and He will heal you.

Don't listen to the voice that chides, "Well, you don't need to be at the service tonight. After all, you were at the church for a committee meeting yesterday. The Lord will understand."

No! If you are in the helps ministry, you should be present at every service because you are an example that others will observe and follow; you have made a commitment to the Lord; and it is vital that you continue to grow spiritually as you are involved in the Ministry of Helps.

You may ask, "But what about my job? I'm required to work every Sunday night."

God fully understands that you must have employment. You need to pray, however, that you will either be given the schedule you desire or that God will give you a new job.

Remember! You should make every effort to be in church when the doors are open.

Three: Be on time.

Promptness and reliability are the hallmarks of a successful ministry.

God created a world of order and that is how He

expects us to conduct our lives. Excuses won't do. You are to be on time for meetings, activities and services.

On several occasions, I've heard people arriving late to assignments apologize, using traffic delays as their excuse.

After years of ministry, I've come to the conclusion that one excuse is as good as another. If believers mean business with God they will keep their appointments.

What is the best way to avoid being late? *Plan to arrive early.*

If you have a 7:00 p.m. meeting, arrive at least 20 or 30 minutes early. As I have said to my members:

> ***"If you run in at 6:59 p.m., you're late! You didn't have time to pray. You didn't have time for instructions. You didn't have time to prepare. You're late!"***

Also plan to arrive early for the main services. People know you are in the helps ministry and they make a mental note every time you walk into a service after it has begun.

If you can't make a commitment to be punctual, don't get involved in ministry.

At Billy Graham's crusade in our city, more than 300,000 people attended the four services. The stadium was more than half filled a few minutes after the gates opened — 90 minutes before the service. More important, the entire crusade staff was there and ready to receive them.

The moment you are in leadership or in the Ministry of Helps, you are essentially saying, "I'm an example. I'm a role model. I help set the pace around here."

Are you ready for that challenge? If so, one of the first places you need to look is at your watch!

Four: You must be a tither.

In our church we have a system for approving people before they can become involved in the Ministry of Helps. Various department heads submit to me or my designee names to be considered for roles in the ministry.

I immediately turn the names over to our record keeping department with these three questions:

1. Are they members of the church?
2. Are they tithing?
3. Have they completed their Ministry of Helps classes?

Invariably, the list will come back with a notation that some person who has been recommended is not a tither — even though he or she may have been a member of the church for two or three years!

How can a church use individuals who fail to honor God with their finances?

Tithing is not an option, it is a command. The Lord

asks, "Will a man rob God? Yet ye have robbed me. But ye say, Wherein have we robbed thee? In tithes and offerings" (Malachi 3:8). God says, "Bring ye all the tithes into the storehouse" (v.10).

Occasionally, when I was about to share with our congregation a vision that required financial support, I first shared it with the leadership — those involved as helpers. For example, recently I told a group, "We are getting ready to present something to the church and we want some of you to pray about becoming vocal or visible in presenting this challenge."

I can turn to them with such assurance because they are faithful supporters of the church and I can call on any of them to encourage the congregation in the area of giving.

God does not send you to a ministry to be idle, but to be active and supportive — in prayer, in service and in giving. "Whatsoever thy hand findeth to do, do it with thy might" (Ecclesiastes 9:10). That means your total support.

Again, let me say this gently, yet firmly. If you are involved in the Ministry of Helps, you must be a tither.

Five: Keep your family in order.

How can you effectively serve God if there is constant strife in your marriage — bickering, arguing and talk about separation and divorce?

In many cases I advise people to stay on the sidelines until certain issues in their families have been resolved.

Here's what Paul wrote to Timothy concerning qualifications for leadership in ministry. The person "must be blameless, the husband of one wife, vigilant, sober, of good behavior, given to hospitality, apt to teach; not given to wine, no striker, not greedy of filthy lucre; but patient, not a brawler, not covetous" (1 Timothy 3:2-3).

Paul continued: "One that ruleth well his own house, having his children in subjection with all gravity; (For if a man know not how to rule his own house, how shall he take care of the church of God?)" (vv.4-5).

Is it too much to expect husbands to love their wives and wives to love their husbands? Both should work toward the same objective and unite around involvement in the church.

I believe the Lord is pleased when He sees a husband and wife team working together in the Ministry of Helps. It creates harmony in the home and is a blessing to the work of God.

It is also important that your children are moving in a spiritual direction.

If there are serious problems in your home, don't hesitate to ask for a leave of absence from your post of ministry. Until the issues are settled, it is better not to put up a false front and live a lie before members of the congregation. However, you should never, never leave the church. Sit under the Word and minister to your family until peace is restored. Get counseling from your pastor if you need to.

What about those who are single? You are expected to live a life submitted to the Word — not someone who is partying, smoking and drinking.

How can you expect to provide the help a ministry requires if you are spending your time in bars and chasing those of the opposite sex?

As examples, we must not only believe, but *behave!*

Six: Go the extra mile.

I've met scores of people who have the attitude: "I'm ready to go home right after church. Please don't ask me to do anything extra."

Have they forgotten that Christ carried the cross to Calvary? He died and was buried for them. Don't they understand that He went to the grave and rose again that we might have life?

The least we can do after accepting Christ into our heart is to become involved in His work and be willing to go the extra mile.

The moment you become active in the Ministry of Helps you should say, "I'm going to give *more* than is expected. I'm going to *add* my gifts to the church and be willing to go to any extreme for God."

The Word says that you are to "Love the Lord thy God with all thy heart, and with all thy soul, and with all thy mind" (Matthew 22:37).

What is "all?" Everything you possess. It's a total commitment — 101 %.

I believe every Christian should view being active in ministry an honor and a delight. It goes far beyond sitting in a pew week after week. If you truly desire to serve the Lord and His church, ask the Father what area you should become involved in. Until you know your area of ministry, find a need and fill it. However, don't stop there! Go the extra mile.

Are You Ready?

The time has come for your talents, skills and abilities to be mightily used in God's Kingdom. You can be part of fulfilling the vision to reach your community and the world.

If you want to touch God, place your hands in what He is doing.

Without hesitation I can tell you that being a

participant in the Ministry of Helps will bring miracles to your life.

> Are you ready to become help that knows the
>   voice of God?
> Are you willing to serve as unto the Lord?
> Are you prepared to be faithful?
> Are you committed to excellence?
> Are you ready to get your pastor's spirit?

If you can answer "Yes," to these questions, the Lord will use you in a miraculous way.

Every ministry needs help! Every ministry needs the right kind of help! Let it be you!

ABOUT THE AUTHOR

Robyn Gool is the founder and Pastor of Victory Christian Center, Charlotte, North Carolina. He is an international teacher, conference keynoter and a distinguished motivational speaker. He has traveled extensively throughout the United States and to a number of countries teaching, preaching, and working with great men and mentors such as Dr. Oral Roberts, Dr. Fred Price, Terry Mize, and the late Dr. Lester Sumrall.

Robyn Gool is founder and President of *More Than Conquerors College*, a school committed to raising leaders for the ministry and society. He is also the founder and senior administrator of *Victory Christian Center School*, a K-3 thru 12 Christian Academy where several hundred students are being trained to excel spiritually and academically.

He is a graduate of Oral Roberts University and was awarded an honorary doctorate from Indiana Christian University.

God has called Robyn Gool to teach principles for success and inspire people to change their circumstances and those of others. To fulfill this call, he and his associate ministers teach and preach a minimum of eight services each week at Victory Christian Center. The message is also presented through daily and weekly television programs seen in North and South Carolina. The ministry owns a television station and three radio stations for the purpose of reaching people with the gospel.

God has also given Robyn Gool a vision to impact his city. To fulfill this vision his ministry owns an apartment complex, several single family homes and a multi-purpose complex which are used to minister to people in need and to meet the needs of the inner city. The ministry also administers the "Super Saturday" program which ministers to the spirit, soul, and body of several hundred inner city children throughout the year. The ministry also sponsors a Shelter Program where homeless individuals are transported, churched, fed and clothed as needed each Sunday.

Robyn Gool is the author of several widely-acclaimed books including *Proper Attitudes Toward Leadership, For Singles Only,* and *From Pressure to Praise.*

The principles in *Every Ministry Needs Help* have been put into practice and are making an impact in Victory Christian Center and across America. He is supported by a staff of capable ministers and has built a contingent of committed leaders that serve him and the ministry with excellence and zeal. Because of the success and excellence of his ministry, Robyn Gool mentors a number of pastors and has become a "pastor's pastor."

Robyn Gool and his wife, Marilyn have three children, Johms, Joi and Sanchia.

OTHER BOOKS BY
ROBYN GOOL

For order information write

CONQUERORS PUBLISHING

P.O. Box 240433, Charlotte, NC 28224

Phone: (704) 527-8181   FAX: (704) 527-8515

NOTES

_____

_____

_____

_____

_____

_____

_____

_____

_____

_____

_____

_____

_____

_____